The Salvation
School For Officers
Library
Chicago

D1624617

Words of
Silver
and Gold

BY JO PETTY
*My Lamp and My Light*
*Words of Silver and Gold*

# Jo Petty

# Words of Silver and Gold

**FLEMING H. REVELL COMPANY**

*Old Tappan, New Jersey*

3606570019 2264

Scripture quotations in this volume are from
the King James Version of the Bible.

*Library of Congress Cataloging in Publication Data*

Words of silver and gold.

    1.  Meditations.  I.  Petty, Jo.
BV4832.2.W67        242'.4       77-23121
ISBN 0-8007-0867-9

Copyright © 1977 by Fleming H. Revell Company
All Rights Reserved
Printed in the United States of America

# Contents

*Words of*
**Silver**
*and* **Gold**

# Preface

Papa reads The Book too, but we hear little of
Whistler's father, Grandpa Moses or Lord Godiva.

If life can only be written by personal knowledge,
I think I qualify. I have been married for fifty years
to the man who inspired this compilation of wise sayings.

I can thoroughly depend upon Papa. His character is
based on principle and the fear of God.

The words that he spoke were not heard by the world at
the time, but now they may be.

Anything that does Papa's heart good, he hastens to
pass on.

If a poet is one who loves and feels great truths, and tells
them, then Papa is a poet.

To know Papa and to love him is a liberal education.

Mankind is better because Papa lives.

JO PETTY

# Words of
# Silver
# and Gold

*Words of*
***Silver***
*(and*$Gold$

# Love

*Papa said—*

Words convey the mental treasures of one period to the generations that follow.

Why are not more gems from our great authors scattered over the country? Great works are not in everybody's reach, and it is better to know them thoroughly than to know them only here and there. It is a good work to give a little to those who have neither time nor means to get more.

There is but one race—the human race.

If God is your Father, man is your brother.

There is no brotherhood of man without the Fatherhood of God.

The brotherhood of man is an integral part of Christianity no less than the Fatherhood of God; to deny one is no less infidel than to deny the other.

The spirit of brotherhood is the healer of the world.

God to love and serve with all my heart, soul, mind and strength, and as myself to love my neighbor!

Christianity is the religion of loving, speaking, and doing, as well as believing.

Christianity [love] feeds the hungry, clothes the naked, visits the sick and the prisoners and seeks the lost.

To love what is good and not to do it when it is possible, is in reality not to love it.

> I sought my soul,
> But my soul I could not see.
>
> I sought my God,
> But my God eluded me.
>
> I sought my brother,
> And I found all three.

The love of our neighbor is the only door out of the dungeon of self.

The lack of love is the most monstrous of all the vices.

Is the likeness of Christ's love easily discernible in me?

Christians [like Christ] base all human relationships in love.

When you love someone, you love him as he is.

Love the sinner but hate and oppose the sin.

Love of God, if it is true and valid, will manifest itself in love of neighbor.

Correction does much, but encouragement does more.

Encouragement after censure is as the sun after a shower.

There is no less eloquence in the voice, the eyes, the gestures, than in words.

Smile when you point out my errors to me.

When the heart is won, the understanding is easily convinced.

Meditate on another's woe and you soon lose your own.

Joining in the amusements of others is, in our social state, the next thing to sympathy in their distresses.

Mature love will bloom with fragrance in every season of life and sweeten the loneliness of declining years.

If you can always love, you will never grow old.

Light up a fire of love in your heart.

Charity is love in action.

The place of charity is everywhere.

Every action motivated by love is of God.

Consider what we are doing and why we are doing it.

Stop playing games with God.

You have not set your own house in order if you are unmindful of your neighbor's well-being.

Jesus Christ put love above all else, a love which is available to all and can overcome evil.

If we honor Christ, it is by the things we do today.

We do not honor God by doing things tomorrow.

All children are our children.

Blow, wind of God, and set us free from hate and want of love.

Charity begins at home.

Charity goes abroad.

It is easy to love those to whom you have done good.

Love considers the well-being of others as important as those of its own.

The only intrinsic evil is a lack of love.

The world is full of beauty when the heart is full of love.

Love is near and prayer is heard.

One loving spirit sets another on fire.

Love needs no teaching nor precept.

Love is never lost. If not reciprocated, it will flow back and soften and purify the heart.

If I love, I have God in me, for God is love.

No sound ought to be heard in the Church but the healing voice of Christian charity.

Preach each sermon as though you will never preach again.

Preach as a dying man to dying men.

More fire in the pulpit—less in the range.

Let us wait on the Lord rather than wait on tables.

> May we be filled with the Holy Ghost
> rather than stuffed with stew or roast.

Ice cream can chill the fervor of spiritual life.

Fewer dinners and more prayer meetings for sinners—us.

The most important thing you can do is love God so much that His love flows into you so much that it fills you so full it splashes out onto every person you meet.

That name of love the Father has bestowed upon us is that we should be called the sons of God!

The responsibility of the Church is to tell of a Divine judgment that requires repentance and a Divine mercy that makes repentance possible.

Love cannot be forced or coerced—it is free to make a choice.

Eyes will not see when the heart wishes them to be blind.

The world needs men and women with the will to labor.

> Not one holy day, but seven,
> Worshiping, not at the call of a bell,
> But at the call of my soul.
> Singing, not at the baton's sway,
> But to the rhythm of my heart.
> Loving, because I must,
> Giving, because I cannot keep,
> Doing for the love of it.

O God, teach me to respect myself as You respect me;
teach me to accept myself as You accept me;
teach me to forgive myself as You forgive me;
teach me to love myself as You love me;
and teach me to love my neighbor as myself.

God permits trials not to impair us, but to improve us.

Ain't we tetchy?

Our first love and our last love is self-love.

Are you more in love with your own opinion or with truth?

He that is not open to conviction is not qualified for discussion.

Men need each other and should love one another and bear each other's burdens.

To find fault is easy; to do better may be difficult.

Those who look for beauty will find it.

Love is the hardest lesson, but for that reason, it should be most our care to learn it.

The heart that is soonest awake to the flowers is the first to be touched by the thorns.

Close your ear against he that opens his mouth against another. If you receive not his words, they fly back and wound him. If you receive them, they flee forward and wound you.

Nothing in this world bears the meek impress of the Son of God so surely as forgiveness.

We are never so beautiful as when we are praying for forgiveness or when forgiving another.

It is easier for the generous to forgive than for the offender to ask forgiveness.

They who forgive most shall be most forgiven.

Refinement that carries us away from one's fellowman is not God's refinement.

Extend the olive branch or you may end up out on a limb.

Regret is the cancer of life. Forgive and then you can forget and have no regret.

Love does not keep a record of wrongs.

> A million times better to forgive than
> Quarrel and wrangle
> And get in a tangle
> Until the old devil
> Drags us down to his level.

"I can forgive, but I cannot forget" is only another way of saying "I will not forgive."

To love an enemy is the distinguished characteristic of the Christian.

No one can forgive my enemy but myself.

May we know our sin which needs forgiving.

May we have the love which can forgive.

Forgiveness requires a power outside ourselves.

Prayer is the key that unlocks the door of forgiveness.

He who loves most is the best and wisest.

Though weary, love is not tired.

The reach of love is greater than we are.

Love fails not.

> He who walks in love may wander far,
> Yet God will bring him where the blessed are.

Give me love and work.

The treasures of the deep are not so precious as are the concealed comforts of a man locked up in a woman's love.

In marriage you are more merry and more sad—fuller of sorrows and fuller of joys.

There are more burdens in marriage, but they are
supported by the strength of love.

Believe in marriage as you believe in the immortality of the
soul.

> You can't leave love to luck.
> Love first may come
> With leaping ecstasy.
> But when ecstasy passes,
> As it always may,
> Love, too, will go
> Unless you make it stay.

The most essential element in any home is God.

Houses are built to live in, more than to look at.

Where there is true love, ceremony is not necessary.

The most influential of all educational factors is the
conversation in a child's home.

> If there has come into your home
> A babe that needs much special care,
> Receive with love that little one
> As if God sent the Christ Child there.

The nearest way to God leads through love's open door.

Our children are only loaned to us.

From her baby the mother learns patience, self-control and endurance.

Help your child to help himself.

Light is the task where many share the toil.

Where God guides, He provides.

Life is ever lord of death, and love can never lose its own.

Love cannot save life from death, but love can fulfill life's purpose.

The answer is love.

> This is our poverty, Lord,
> We don't belong to each other
> Or serve one another.
> We each go our own way
> And do not care for our neighbor.
> O Lord, redeem us
> From this estrangement.

Our life is like the dial of a clock.
The hands are God's hands, passing over and over again.
The short hand is the hand of discipline,
The long hand is the hand of mercy.

Slowly and surely the hand of discipline must pass
And God speaks at each stroke;
But over and over passes the hand of mercy,
Showering down sixtyfold of blessings for each
Stroke of discipline or trial,
And both hands are fastened to one secure pivot,
The great, unchanging heart of a God of love.
(Papa is a retired watchmaker.)

# Joy

*Papa said—*

A few useful wise sayings at hand do more toward a wise and happy life than whole volumes of caution we know not where to find.

When you read a wise saying, take it for your own and make immediate application of it.

Truth is the property of no individual, but is the treasure of all.

Meditate on these sayings until the truth in them becomes your own and part of your being.

Light another person's candle by your own and you will not lose any of the brilliancy by what the other gains.

Enjoy the present moment.

Make a habit of being happy.

Everything you want is within yourself.

Make your work your amusement.

Labor gives relish to pleasure.

Employment is nature's physician.

Employment is essential to happiness.

Every person's task is his life preserver.

Success or failure in business is caused more by the mental attitudes than by mental capacities.

Happiness does not come from easy work so much as from a difficult task which requires our very best.

Work is a necessary duty.

Rust rots the steel which use preserves.

Heartaches are but stepping-stones to nobler living, greater insight, compassion and understanding.

I can continue my work, even my joys, in the presence of my greatest grief.

What can winter do if spring is in my heart?

Life is a preparation for eternity.

May I spread the message our Master taught!

Delight in praising God.

If you would first pause to thank God for every pleasure, For mourning over grief you would not find the leisure.

To love Jesus is happiness!

The meaning of Christmas is for every day and every man.

By the time we count only a few of our blessings, we shall be praising the Lord for His goodness and mercy and love.

Sorrow is only one of the lower notes in the oratorio of our blessedness.

> We sorrow not as others do
> Whose joy fades like the flowers.
> There is a hope that's born of God
> And such a hope is ours.

Let gratitude for the past inspire us with trust for the future.

Seek happiness not in the future, but at your feet.

We have no sorrow that God cannot heal.

Wealth proves how little we really enjoy this world.

Be glad for little things.

Cheerful looks make every dish a feast.

Of all the good things we can acquire, we enjoy only as much as we can use.

Want of desire is great riches.

Give us the poverty that enjoys true wealth.

Search for wisdom as for hidden treasures.

The love of knowledge comes with reading and grows thereby.

Books are a guide in youth and an entertainment for age.

Great books are the medicines of the soul.

Books, like friends, should be few and well chosen. Like friends, we should return to them again and again, and like true friends they will never fail us.

Except a living person, there is nothing more wonderful than a good book.

A good book is the best of friends.

Be as careful of the books you read as the company you keep.

Classic literature is always modern.

A knowledge of the Bible would improve all the relations of social and domestic life.

The highest of earthly enjoyment is but a shadow of the joy to be found in reading the Bible.

We cannot be well educated without a knowledge of the Bible.

From God comes knowledge and understanding.

A wise man will increase learning.

Few things are needed to make the wise happy.

The principles of the Bible are the groundwork of human freedom.

He is free whom the truth makes free—all others are slaves.

The spirit of liberty is respect for the rights of others and unwillingness for anyone to be wronged.

True liberty can never interfere with the duties, rights and interests of others.

Liberty implies duty rather than privilege.

Thank God for the right to hope, to dream, and to pray, and then remember the obligation to serve.

Selfishly seek happiness for yourself and it will elude you. Spend your life in seeking to serve others, asking no recognition or reward, and you will be happy.

Enjoy yourself.

Our home joys are the most delightful earth affords.

It's incredible when you think about it, how little our parents knew about child psychology, yet how wonderful we turned out.

Know ye not that children usually turn out pretty well in spite of their parents?

When parents spoil children, is it to please the children or please themselves?

An infallible way to make your child miserable is to satisfy all his desires.

Happiness grows at your own fireside and is not picked up in strangers' gardens.

True happiness is found in the home where love and trust increase with the years.

Domestic happiness is the end of almost all our pursuits.

A prince wants only the pleasures of private life to complete his happiness.

The clasp of a hand and a winning smile do a lot to make life worth while.

A good laugh is sunshine in the house.

A good conscience is a continual Christmas.

There is no greater everyday virtue than cheerfulness.

Wondrous is the strength of cheerfulness.

I was made to enjoy as well as to labor.

We enjoy thoroughly only the pleasure that we give.

The luxury of doing good surpasses every other personal enjoyment.

To find happiness by changing anything is to change your own disposition.

You travel the world in search of happiness, when a contented mind is within reach of every person.

He who loses anything and gets wisdom by it is a gainer by the loss.

If all but yourself were blind, would you want a fine home and fine furniture?

Reputation makes you rich or poor. Character makes you happy or sad.

Refrain from covetousness and your estate shall prosper.

The covetous man is up to his chin in water and yet thirsty.

Dream not of some magical rose garden over the horizon instead of enjoying the roses that are blooming outside your window today.

Be it ever so humble, there's no place like home.

The bosom can ache beneath diamond brooches.

How many toil to lay up riches they never enjoy!

A rich dress adds but little to the beauty of a person.

If clothes do make the man, I'm mighty glad I have some.

Money is not required to buy one necessity of the soul.

> Honour the Lord with thy substance, and with the
> firstfruits of all thine increase: So shall thy barns be
> filled with plenty, and thy presses shall burst out with
> new wine.
> *Proverbs 3:9, 10*

Work is as much a necessity as eating and sleeping.

Whatever is worth doing at all is worth doing well.

The day shall not be up so soon as I, to try the fair
adventure of tomorrow.

One dog does not exchange his bone with another dog.

The fruit that can fall without shaking the tree is too
mellow for me.

Every person is unique.

Play your part well.

It is a most slavish thing to luxuriate, and a most royal thing to labor.

I love to hear one singing at his work.

To cultivate a garden is to walk with God.

Lovely flowers are the smile of God's goodness.

All great art is the expression of man's delight in God's work.

Forgiveness is the most necessary and proper work of every man.

Why deny yourself the pleasure of forgiving your enemy or one who has offended you?

The narrow soul knows not the Godlike glory of forgiving.

The joy comes with the second mile.

Old age is a blessed time. It gives us leisure to put off our earthly garments one by one and dress ourselves for heaven.

Childhood itself is scarcely more lovely than a cheerful, kindly, sunshiny old age.

If you would be beautiful, scatter joy.

The highest wisdom is continual cheerfulness.

Happy are those whose later years are not a footnote to life but an interesting last chapter.

As you grow older, your eyes grow weaker so that when you look into the mirror you look just as beautiful as ever.

We live in deeds, not years; in thoughts, not breaths.

We feel our age by the strength of our soul rather than the weakness of our body.

God has given us memories that we may enjoy roses in December.

Happy is the person who so lives that at all times death may find him at leisure to die.

Keep me young enough to laugh with little children and understanding enough to appreciate how it is when you get old.

A sense of humor helps to reduce your troubles to where you can handle them.

Judicious praise is to children what the sun is to flowers.

As for parents, our praises are our wages.

He who remembers the benefits of his parents is too much occupied to remember their faults.

May you grow old gracefully and happily.

For the ignorant, old age is as winter; for the learned, it is a harvest.

Age is not all decay; it is the ripening, the swelling of the fresh life within, that withers and bursts the husk.

Our faith is defective if old age is not a season of hopeful prospect—not sad retrospect.

Since we receive mercies constantly, gratitude to God should be habitual.

Our thanks should be as fervent for mercies received as our petitions for mercies sought.

We enjoy the true taste of life when we are ready and willing to quit it.

We complain that our days are few and act as though there would be no end of them.

The expectation of always living here and living thus would indeed be a prospect of overwhelming despair.

There is pleasure enough in this life to make us wish to live, and pain enough to reconcile us to death when we can live no longer.

Let your religion be seen—lamps shine.

To be happy ourselves is a most effectual contribution to the happiness of others.

Joy has her tears.

He that thinks he is happy, is.

Happiness can be built only on virtue and must of necessity have truth for its foundation.

The beauty seen is partly in him who sees it.

No man is hurt but by himself.

Practice an attitude of gratitude.

Happiness in the world begins in the home with *you*.

Unhappy because this has happened to me?
No, I am happy though this has happened to me.

Birds sing every day.

Joy is love with its hand to the plow.

"Mean to" don't pick no cotton.

# Peace

*Papa said—*

A truth is as comfortable in homely language as in fine speech.

The greatest learning is to be seen in the greatest plainness.

There is a want of the heart which all creation cannot supply.

None but God can satisfy the longings of the immortal soul.

The best of man's wisdom will fail to satisfy the deeper longings of the soul.

The philosophies of man have failed to meet the basic needs of man.

Our basic physical needs are simple—a little food, sun, air, water, shelter, warmth and sleep.

> But whoso hearkeneth unto me [wisdom] shall dwell safely, and shall be quiet from fear of evil.
>
> Proverbs 1:33

A fool despises wisdom and instruction.

The wise man can find no rest in that which perishes.

> . . . thy rod and thy staff they comfort me.
>
> Psalms 23:4

Repose can only be found in everlasting principles.

The end of doubt is the beginning of repose.

We can never be fully satisfied but in God.

There is little peace or comfort in life if we are always anxious as to future events.

The fear of ill exceeds the ill we fear.

Do not clog your happiness with care, destroying what *is* with thoughts of what *may be.*

Cast your care upon God. There is no merit in walking burdened.

No person is strong enough to carry today's duties with tomorrow's anxieties.

Never trouble trouble till trouble troubles you.

Early and provident fear is the mother of safety.

Put off your cares with your clothes, so you may sleep well.

Do not distress yourself with imaginings.

The secret of peace is the constant referral of all our anxieties to God.

Rx—Relax

Use three physicians: Dr. Quiet, Dr. Diet and Dr. Merryman.

If we have not peace within ourselves, it is in vain to seek it from outward sources.

By all means, take some time to be alone; see what your soul wears; dare to look in your chest, and tumble up and down what you find there.

You are never less alone than when alone.

Desire only the will of God; seek Him alone and supremely and you will find peace.

> . . . learn of me [Jesus] . . . and ye shall find rest unto your souls. For my yoke is easy, and my burden is light.
> Matthew 11:29, 30

If your burden is heavy, question if God has placed the burden upon you!

God is present everywhere and every person is His work.

Anxiety is the rust of life, destroying it.

It is worse to apprehend than to suffer.

Some of the worst evils are those that never arrive.

The root of all discontent is self-love.

The more self is indulged, the more it demands.

Of all men, the selfish are most discontented.

Fear no man so much as yourself.

Other than God, be fearful only of yourself.

You may avoid another enemy, but you can never avoid yourself.

It is easy to be content and at peace if our conscience is pure.

Labor to keep alive in your heart that celestial fire called conscience. If conscience smites you once, it is an admonition; if twice, it is a condemnation.

There is no witness so terrible—no accused so powerful— as conscience which dwells within us.

The voice of conscience is so delicate that it is easy to stifle it; but it is also so clear that it is impossible to mistake it.

Conscience is man's most faithful friend.

Stand in awe of none but your own conscience.

The still small voice of conscience cannot be drowned by the loud noise of revelry.

Conscience tells me if I do wrong and approves if I do right.

A quiet conscience makes one so serene.

A man without decision is as a wave of the sea—a feather in the air, which every breeze blows about as it pleases.

A place for everything—everything in its place.

A time and place for everything. Do everything in its turn and place, and you will accomplish more and have more leisure, too.

One who is afraid of lying is usually afraid of nothing else.

Be always content with what happens, for know that which God chooses is better than what you choose.

He who strives not to please men and fears not to displease them shall enjoy much peace.

Many people agree without being aware of it—they have merely used different words to state their opinions.

Do we fear godless nations more than we fear the God of the nations?

The peace of the world will be uncertain unless we keep the peace of God.

> Home, the spot of earth supremely blest,
> A dearer, sweeter spot than all the rest.

Is your home a place of rest and refreshment, where God Himself becomes more real to those who enter?

He that has little and wants less is richer than he that has much and wants more.

He is not rich that possesses much, but he that covets no more.

The discontented are never rich.

Contentment is natural wealth.

If you are but content, you have enough to live upon with comfort.

He who is not contented with what he has would not be contented with what he would like to have.

A contented mind is a great treasure.

Luxury is artificial poverty.

The contented man is never poor.

Gray hairs seem to my fancy like the soft light of the moon, silvery over the evening of life.

Evening is the delight of virtuous age. It seems an emblem of the tranquil close of a busy life—serene, placid, and mild.

Many angels tho unseen are around us when we sleep or wake.

> Content can soothe where'er by God placed;
> Can raise a garden in the desert waste.

> More safe am I with Your hand
> Than if a host did round me stand.

Why should we fear to tread the path to our future home?

Let not our babbling dreams affright our souls.

Our piety must be weak and imperfect if we do not conquer the fear of death.

Blessed are they that are homesick, for they shall get home.

Contentment in God's will is the best remedy we can apply to misfortunes.

There is peace in an accepted sorrow.

To strive with any destroys my peace.

Let there be peace on earth and let it begin with me.

May my God be your God.
May your refuge and your comfort be as great as mine.

Lo! God is here and we knew it not.

# Long-suffering (Patience)

*Papa said—*

A thing is never too often repeated which is never sufficiently learned.

It is not enough to cram ourselves with a great load of collections of proverbs—we must chew them over and over again.

We need to be constantly reminded of those things we constantly forget.

So have at it with a proverb.

God had one Son on earth without sin, but never one without suffering.

. . . despise not the chastening of the Lord; neither be weary of his correction: For whom the Lord loveth he correcteth; even as a father the son in whom he delighteth.

Proverbs 3:11, 12

Blessed is the discipline that causes me to reach out for a closer union with Jesus.

From our errors and mistakes we learn wisdom for the future.

Experience is a great education.

Never permit errors to discourage you.

He only is exempt from failures who makes no efforts.

He conquers who endures.

Hardships teach fortitude.

It is not help, but obstacles, that make men.

Not failure, but low aim is a crime.

It is not the leap at the start but the steady going that gets you there.

Man will not learn from the suffering of others; he must suffer himself.

We know nothing truly that we have not learned from experience.

The world is God's workshop for making men.

Know how sublime a thing it is to suffer and be strong.

Bumps and bruises and turbulence are part of the price you pay for life's richness.

God teaches us by our experiences.

It lightens the stroke when I draw near to God, who handles the rod.

I shall not escape censure, and if I am affected by it, that is a weakness.

Occasions do not make a man frail, but show what he is.

If you would gain power and strength to overcome the temptations of the enemy, be a person of prayer.

Early adversity is often a blessing.

Man judges us by the success of our efforts. God looks on the efforts themselves.

We must be disappointed with the lesser things of life to comprehend the full value of the greater.

Every tear is a cleansing virtue.

Keep on keeping on.

Conquer yourself.

Be patient with life, for it is eternal.

*Now* is eternity.

Living out our years teaches us kindness, gentleness and meekness.

The end of life is to be like God, and the soul following God will be like Him.

Life does not need comfort when it can be offered meaning, nor pleasure when it can be shown purpose.

Be patient with yourself—God is.

Difficulties show men what they are.

The true worker in any sphere is continually coping with difficulties.

Difficulties are a compliment from God—a proof of confidence in us.

Be like the reed which bends to every breeze, but breaks not in the tempest.

A house built on the sand is in fair weather just as good as if built on a rock.

The illusion that the times that *were* are better than those that *are* has probably pervaded all ages.

By neglecting small matters, the soul becomes accustomed to unfaithfulness.

Take time enough for the most trivial deed.

Genius begins great works; labor alone finishes them.

Excellence in any department can be attained only by the labor of a lifetime.

The best education in the world is that gotten by struggling to get a living.

One is wise if he can gain wisdom by observing the experiences of another.

Never complain about your troubles—they are responsible for more than half your income.

> My competitors sometimes do as much for me as do my friends. My friends are too polite to point out my weaknesses, but my competitors go to great length to advertise them.
>
> My competitors are efficient, diligent and attentive. They make me search continually for ways to improve my service.
>
> My competitors would take some business away from me if they could. This keeps me alert to hold what I have, and to go after even more.
>
> My competitors prevent me from becoming lazy, incompetent and careless. I need the discipline they enforce upon me.
>
> My competitors deserve the highest praise. They have been good to me.

The slander of some people is as great a recommendation as the praise of others.

Neglected slander soon expires; show that you are hurt and you give it the appearance of truth.

Doing the will of God leaves me no time to complain.

There are strange contradictions in human character.

Whatever we blame in another we can find in our own heart.

To persevere in one's duty and be silent is the best answer to slander.

What you dislike in another, take care to correct in yourself.

We think the trouble is with the other fellow.

He censures God who quarrels with the imperfections of men.

He surely is most in need of another's patience who has none of his own.

If I were kicked by a mule, I would not think of kicking the mule back.

Strive not to silence your opponent so much as to convince him.

If people are unwilling to hear you, better to hold your tongue.

Consider how you often suffer more from your anger and grief than from the things that anger and grieve you.

. . . Vengeance is mine; I will repay, saith the Lord.
Romans 12:19

It is to the glory of a man to pass over a transgression.

I see in you no fault that I could not have committed myself.

Why is that we "upbraid" others in reproving them, instead of "downbraiding"?

And why "shortcomings," but no "longcomings"?

A pint can't hold a quart.

It is easy to bear the misfortune of others like a Christian.

The silver lining is easier to find in someone else's cloud.

> Thought is the blossom,
> Language the bud,
> Action the fruit.

I have never heard anything about the resolutions of the Apostles, but a good deal about their acts.

The family is the great discipline, where each generation learns anew that no man can live for himself alone.

The best school of discipline is home and family. Home life is God's own method of training the young; and homes are very much what women make them.

Nursery school is where small children go to catch colds from each other so they can stay home.

There's nothing wrong with teenagers that reasoning with them won't aggravate.

As the twig is bent, the tree is inclined.

The apple does not fall far from the tree.

No gains without pains.

If we never have headaches from rebuking our children, we shall have plenty of heartaches when they grow up.

We never give our children a lift when we give them a free ride.

There are more than three R's:

Readin', Ritin', Rithmetic;
Respect, Religion, Responsibility;
Riot, Restlessness, Rebellion;
Ruin, Rot, Regret.

He who best governs himself is best fitted to govern others.

An angry man is again angry with himself when he returns to reason.

Contemplation is to knowledge what digestion is to food.

Contemplation will strengthen for action, and action sends us back for more meditation.

Ask God for what we need—watch and labor for all that we ask.

Wait, I say, wait on the Lord.

Be not idle while waiting.

> . . . they that wait upon the Lord shall renew their strength; they shall mount up with wings as eagles; they shall run, and not be weary; and they shall walk, and not faint.
>
> Isaiah 40:31

Be patient with one another and with ourselves.

Patience smiles and bears.

The one you influence today may grow up to influence a hundred thousand people.

Men are likely to settle a question rightly if it is discussed freely.

The mechanic that would perfect his work must first sharpen his tools.

Be thankful for the possession and be patient in the loss.

What would the nightingale care if the toad despised her singing?

To keep your secret is wisdom, but to expect others to keep it is folly.

Never chase a lie; if you let it alone, it may soon run itself to death.

Wanna forget all your other troubles? Wear tight shoes.

When your nose is stopped up, all you want to do is breathe. Right?

For every bad there might be a worse.

Do you get mad when you stub your toe?
Thank God you have a toe to stub.

Now that I'm old, it does not upset me one whit to step out of the shower and find the mirror fogged up.

Growing old is only a state of mind brought on by gray hair, false teeth, wrinkles, a large belly, short breath, and an all-over feeling of being constantly and totally pooped.

One can get used to anything but hanging.

Run when you can. Walk when you cannot run. Creep when you cannot walk.

When your voice is too weak to praise God, praise Him in your sighs.

In love's service only the wounded can serve.

He has half the deed done who has made a beginning.

I will chide no one but myself, against whom I know most faults.

Man is the only animal that can get skinned twice.

Look before you leap.

Beware the fury of a patient man!

Patient, O heart, though heavy be your sorrows;
Be not cast down, disquieted in vain;
Yet shall you praise God when those darkened furrows,
Where now He plows, wave with golden grain.

O Lord, teach me to use all the circumstances of my
life that they may bring forth the fruit of the
Spirit which is Love—Joy—Peace—Long-suffering—
Goodness—Gentleness—Meekness—Temperance—Faith.

# Goodness

*Papa said—*

The time of business does not differ from the time of prayer.

A good man does good merely by living.

How good is God our Father,
Who does all things well!

God is good.

Christ is the perfect representative of God.

God is the source of all goodness.

God became man that man might become like God.

As many as are led by the Spirit of God, they are the sons of God; as many—no more.

The only way we can become more like Jesus is to spend much time with Him—be His intimate friend.

A Christian is nothing but a sinful man who studies the Bible for the honest purpose of becoming better.

Character is man's greatest need and man's greatest safeguard.

A good character is not inherited from parents.

Character cannot be complete without religion.

Hold fast to Christ. Keep Him firm in your motto and your heart, and your character will take care of itself.

Character is what man is in the dark.

Christ has no message nor mission for any other than sinners.

Jesus Christ came into the world to save sinners—that includes me!

The Church is not composed of people who are better than the rest, but of people who are trying to be better than they are; not of people who are perfect, but of people who are dissatisfied with their imperfections.

We all know better than we practice.

We all recognize a better law than we obey.

You cannot have my sins and I cannot have your virtues.

Fear nothing so much as sin.

Conscience tells us that we ought to do right. God's Word teaches us what is right.

To keep your conscience in a state of good repair, keep it enlightened by the Word of God.

Conscience prompts us to do right and warns us against the wrong.

Conscience warns us as a friend before it punishes us as a judge.

A tender conscience is an inestimable blessing; that is, a conscience not only quick to discern what is evil, but instantly to shun it, as the eyelids close themselves against the mote.

Conscience asks only, "Is it right?"

If but one sin force its way into the conscience and is permitted to dwell there, the road is paved for many iniquities.

It is astonishing how soon the whole conscience begins to unravel if a single stitch drops. One sin indulged in makes a hole you could put your head through.

Sin is like a poisoned worm feeding on all the beauty of the soul.

A good conscience never costs as much as it is worth.

If you are not right toward God, you cannot be right toward men.

Christianity is a life—not a theory—not a philosophy of life—but a serious occupation of our whole existence.

Truth does not change with the changing times.

Those who listen for the voice of truth will hear.

Right is right if nobody is right.

Wrong is wrong if everybody is wrong.

> Woe unto them that call evil good, and good evil;
> that put darkness for light, and light for darkness;
> that put bitter for sweet, and sweet for bitter!
> > Isaiah 5:20

All our millions of laws are nothing but so many efforts
to get us to observe the Ten Commandments.

The regulations on speed of our cars is based on God's
commandment "Thou shalt not kill."

A man's word should be as good as his bond.

> Ye shall know them by their fruits. . . .
> > Matthew 7:16

What a man does tells us what he is.

Virtue is the only nobility.

Accuracy of statement is one of the first elements of
truth.

Deceit is a lie put into practice.

If you would be good, first believe you are bad.

> . . . all our righteousnesses are as filthy rags . . . .
> Isaiah 64:6

The fact of evil is clear. Human experience everywhere is marred by it.

We talk as if we believe in God, but live as though there is no God.

This world is made better by every man improving his own conduct; no reform is accomplished wholesale.

True repentance is to cease from sinning.

To do so no more is the truest repentance.

The slightest sorrow for sin is sufficient if it produces amendment, and the greatest sorrow is insufficient if it does not.

When the soul has laid down its faults at the feet of Christ, it feels as though it had wings!

There is a straight fence. There is right and wrong; there is no sitting on that fence.

It is the guilt, not the scaffold, which constitutes the crime.

The conscience is God in the human soul making known the presence of its rightful sovereign, the Giver of truth.

> . . . take not thy holy spirit from me.
> Psalms 51:11

A disciplined conscience is man's most faithful friend.

The doctrines of the Bible involve all moral truth known by man; so extensive are its precepts that they require every virtue and forbid every sin.

If the power of the Gospel is not felt in the length and breadth of the land, anarchy and misrule, degradation and misery, corruption and darkness will reign.

We are in a sad state unless religious books are widely circulated among the masses in this country and our people become religious.

To become a thoroughly good person is the best prescription for keeping a sound mind in a sound body.

To prevent evil is better than to remedy it.

Keep God's law and length of days and peace shall be added to you.

All aspects of life are holy; let us take care not to draw any sharp lines between secular and spiritual life.

Every man is the architect of his own character.

The Christian is the highest style of man.

Morality looks that the skin of the apple be fair; religion searches to the very core.

If we are so wicked with religion, what would we be without it?

Forbear to judge, for we are all sinners.

The deadliest sin is to think we have no sin.

> For the wages of sin is death . . . .
> Romans 6:23

Fear nothing but doing wrong.

No sin is small—it is against an infinite God.

Be sure your sin will find you out.

Sin with the multitude and your responsibility and guilt are as great and as truly personal as if you alone had done the wrong.

Who to himself is law, no law needs.

> Build it well whatever you do,
> Build it straight and strong and true;
> Build it clean and high and broad;
> Build it for the eye of God.

Small deeds done are better than great deeds planned.

That which we are, we are all the while teaching.

Good is best when soonest done.

It is the will that makes the action good or bad.

Teach our children to be not what we are, but what they should be.

Nothing is more important for the country than to train up youth in wisdom and virtue.

A terrible sin is the mutilation of a child's spirit.

> All dust is frail, all flesh is weak.
> You be the true man that you seek.

Be what you desire to appear to be.

Where you are is not important, but only what you are doing there.

Wherever your place—that for you is the post of duty.

Solitude shows us what we should be; society shows us what we are.

Dare to be true; nothing can need a lie.

It requires no extraordinary talents to lie and deceive.

We are never so easily deceived as while we are endeavoring to deceive others.

Children often perceive your slightest defects.

Let honesty be the breath of your soul.

Nothing can be truly great which is not right.

Do as you say; say as you do.

To your own self be true; and it must follow, as the night the day, you cannot then be false to any man.

To change the place does not change the man.

Circumstances obey principles.

Character development should be the aim of education.

A straight line is the shortest path, in morals as well as in geometry.

True honesty renders to God the things which are God's and to man the things that are man's.

A large part of virtue consists of good habits.

There is but one virtue—the eternal sacrifice of self.

The tongue is the instrument of the greatest good and the greatest evil that is done in the world.

> . . . fear the Lord, and depart from evil. It shall be health to thy navel, and marrow to thy bones.
> Proverbs 3:7, 8

Better to bear injustice than do it.

He is armed without, who is innocent within.

We should live the way we pray.

Be as great in your acts as you have been in your thoughts.

The first great gift we can bestow on others is a good example.

So act that your principle of action might safely be made a law for the whole world.

To be doing good is man's most glorious task.

We persuade others by being in earnest ourselves.

Christianity is a life as well as a creed.

Goodness is love in action.

A man's mere word should be his bond.

Live as if you expected to live to be a hundred but might die tomorrow.

We can never be better for our religion if our neighbor is worse for it.

Those who are most perfect have many imperfections.

Behave to all others as you wish they would behave to you.

He that does good to another does good also to himself.

Sacrifice pleasure to duty.

Rather do and not promise than promise and not do.

All men's good; each man's rule.

Evil is wrought by want of thought as well as by want of heart.

Little deeds are great because Christ dwells within us.

When Christ is in us, great deeds are easy because of His power.

Morality does not make a Christian, but one cannot be a Christian without it.

To set a lofty example is the richest bequest a person can leave behind.

Virtue speaks louder than words.

Goodness smiles to the end.

Speak one true word today, and it shall go ringing on through the ages

Do unto others as you would have them do unto you. This is the whole law, the rest is commentary.

The people's safety is the law of God.

Good laws make it easier to do right and harder to do wrong.

False freedom is to do what you like.
True freedom is to do what you ought.

Laws can discover sin but not remove it.

To obey God is perfect liberty.

No man can always do just as he chooses until he chooses to do God's will.

Christianity everywhere gives dignity to labor, sanctity to marriage and brotherhood to man.

He who would be angry and sin not must not be angry with anything but sin.

To pity distress is but human; to relieve it is Christian.

Why help people who don't need help? That doesn't make sense to me.

It is another's fault if he be ungrateful, but it is mine if I do not give.

The true Christian is the true citizen.

There is no solid wisdom but in true piety.

To smile at a jest which plants a thorn in another's breast is to become a principal in the mischief.

There is no liberty in wrongdoing.

Never think you can pursue good by evil means without sinning.

The things we don't do determine the kind of person we are as surely as the things we do.

The truly generous is the truly wise.

Talebearers are just as bad as tale makers.

> For the love of money is the root of all evil . . . .
> 1 Timothy 6:10

We are as near to heaven as we are far from self.

When men cease to be faithful to God, he who expects them to be faithful to each other will be much disappointed.

Our mistakes show us we cannot depend on our wisdom— all wisdom comes from God.

Our failures teach us we have no strength of our own.

It's not the times that are bad, but man.

Many a person thinks it is goodness which keeps him from crime when it is only a full stomach.

Don't mistake potatoes for principles.

Sincerity is no test of truth.

God's Word is the only true standard of decision.

What others say of me matters little, what I say myself matters much.

The brighter your candle burns, the more easily you can light mine.

How far the little candle throws its light!

Delight in goodness.

It is only imperfection that complains of what is imperfect.

No leaf is perfect, but no two are alike.

So long as we are full of self we are shocked at the faults of others.

A song may outlive all sermons in the memory.

That which is good is always beautiful.

Beauty is the mark God sets on virtue.

Around the neck of the beautiful what dross are gold
and pearls.

Let no man value at a little price a virtuous woman's
counsel.

A beautiful woman is a jewel—a good woman is a treasure.

Beauty is nothing where virtue is not.

Pretty is as pretty does.

Beauty without virtue is as a flower without perfume.

It is not enough to do the right thing, it must be done in
the right manner.

Light a thousand torches at one torch and the flame of
the latter remains the same.

Age sours the bad and sweetens the good.

Let your little light shine.

Speak well of everyone if you speak of him at all—none of us is so very good.

Your reputation may be learned in an hour; your character may not come to light for a year or more.

Half-finished tasks do not improve character.

Your reputation may be destroyed by slander. Only you can hurt your character.

If one slanders you, live so that nobody will believe him.

Half a fact is a whole falsehood.

Continue to tell "white lies" and you'll soon be color-blind.

Were I chaste as ice and pure as snow, I shall not escape slander.

I know of more faults in myself than anyone.

Justice delayed is justice denied.

As your behavior is before your children's faces, such is their behavior behind your back.

You should not rebuke in children what they see practiced in you.

Before you beat a child be sure you yourself are not the cause of the offense.

The youngest children are nearest to God.

A child strayed from his duty and returned to it again with tears is conversion.

When a child can be brought to tears from repentance for his offense, he needs no chastisement.

It is wiser to put our attention on the good and the beautiful and dwell as little as possible on the evil and the false.

> . . . if there be any virtue, and if there be any praise, think on these things.
>
> Philippians 4:8

Give as you would receive—cheerfully, quickly.

You cannot build character and courage by taking away a person's initiative and independence.

All good government must begin in the home.

It is useless to make good laws for bad people.

Conscience, though ever so small a worm while we live, grows suddenly into a serpent on our deathbed!

The torture of a bad conscience is the hell of a living soul.

> When at the judgment seat of God
> Whose guilt will greater be?
> The man who threw the dirty clod
> Or the one whose sin you see.

If you are not virtuous, you will become vicious.

> . . . Resist the devil, and he will flee from you.
> James 4:7

One fault of a good man will meet with more reproaches than all his virtues will with praise.

Death first struck Abel, the innocent and righteous.

It is right living which prepares for safe or even joyous death.

Better to suffer wrong than to do it.

Do God's will as if it were your will and God will accomplish your will as if it were His own.

Live before you die as you will wish you had when you come to die.

We pray as Jesus taught us, "Deliver us from evil."

No evil can happen to a good man, either in life before death or life after death.

The heart renewed by Divine grace grows steadily into the likeness of the Divine.

> But the path of the just is as the shining light, that shineth more and more unto the perfect day.
>
> Proverbs 4:18

Keep your nose clean so you can smell a phony.

Words of
*Silver*
*and* **Gold**

# Gentleness

*Papa said—*

The short sayings of wise and good men are of great value.

Wisdom gained by one man is invested in all men and is
a permanent investment for all time.

A sentence may hit home where a sermon does not.

Here are jewels of knowledge which can easily be retained
and transmitted.

The deepest truths are the simplest.

Take delight in simple things.

Be swift to love—make haste to be kind.

None is so near God as he who shows kindness.

Kindness to children and a willingness to conform to the ideal character of childhood are marks of a true Christian.

Kindness is the golden chain by which society is bound together.

Lord, for today make my words gracious and tender; for tomorrow I may have to eat them.

> Any unselfish, kindly deed
> With never a thought of fame
> Becomes a "cup of cold water"
> If given in Jesus' name.

Kind words and helpful deeds, gentle actions and a generous attitude burst out all over true faith like blossoms on well-watered plants.

True politeness is treating others as you love to be treated yourself.

Real kindness kindly expressed is politeness.

We must not contradict, but instruct those that contradict us.

To contradict a statement of an opponent is not proof that you are right.

Small courtesies sweeten life.

Life is not so short but there is always time for courtesy.

To dispense with ceremony is to confer a compliment.

Find happiness in simplicity and in the happiness of others.

True beauty when unadorned is adorned the most.

Simplicity is greatness.

O God, keep us simple.

We hand folks over to God's mercy and show none ourselves.

Christianity undertakes to make men disposed to do right.

Only the Almighty can make a gentleman.

Discipline is a little cruel that it may be very kind.

God has given us hope and sleep as a compensation for the many cares of life.

The light shines in the darkness and the darkness has not overcome it.

The greatness of my stumbling and the multitude of my sins go not beyond the mercy of my God.

The law of judgment is mercy.

> Let not mercy and truth forsake thee: bind them about thy neck; write them upon the table of thine heart: So shalt thou find favour and good understanding in the sight of God and man.
>
> Proverbs 3:3, 4

True greatness is being great in little things.

Have no room in your heart to hold the memory of a wrong.

If the injury began on his part, the kindness must begin on your part.

Pray for a short memory to all unkindnesses.

Mercy is the order of the day in the kingdom of Christ.

We pray for mercy, and that same prayer teaches us to render the deeds of mercy.

Who will not mercy unto others show, how can he mercy ever hope to have?

Mercy to him that shows it is the rule.

> Teach me to feel another's woe,
> To hide the fault I see;
> That mercy I to others show,
> That mercy show to me.

God's mercies are new every morning.

There is no dispute without passion, and yet there is scarcely a dispute worth a passion.

There is a difference between perseverance and obstinacy. One comes from a strong *will*, the other from a strong *won't*.

One drop of water helps to fill the ocean.

Moments make the years.

Never report what may hurt another unless it be a greater hurt to another to cover it.

I did not come to comfort you—only God can do that—but I did come to say how deeply and tenderly I feel for you in your affliction.

Only the truly strong can be tender.

Always be a little kinder than necessary.

Rather never to receive a kindness that never to bestow one.

I have no more right to say an unkind thing than to act one.

If you are gentle and good, the world is better for it.

Hearts are like flowers; they remain open to the softly falling dew, but shut up in the violent downpour of rain.

As I age, I mellow.

All things are possible to one who believes;
they are less difficult to one who hopes;
they are easy to one who loves;
and they are all simple to anyone who does all three.

I called him John, he called me Jim,
Nigh fifty years that I knowed him
And he knowed me; and he was square
An' honest all that time, an' fair.

I'd pass him mornings going down
The road or drivin' into town,
An' we'd look up the same old way,
An' wave a hand and smile an' say:
 "Hello, John,"
 "Hello, Jim."

I guess you don't real often see
Such kind of friends as Jim and me;
Not much at talkin' big; but say,
Th' kind of friends that stick an' stay.
Come rich, come poor, come rain, come shine,
Whatever he might have was mine
And mine was his'n an' we both knowed it
When we'd holler on the road:
 "Howdy, John,"
 "Howdy, Jim."

An' when I got froze out one year
He dropped in on me with that queer
Big smile, upon his way to town
An' layed two hundred dollars down,
An' says: "No intrust, understand,
Er not." An' he took my hand
An' squeezed it an' he druv away
'Cause there wa'n't nothing more to say:
 "S'long, John,"
 "S'long, Jim."

# Meekness

*Papa said—*

To select well among old things is almost equal to inventing new ones.

An apt quotation is as good as an original remark.

The more things change, the more they are the same.

Everything has been said better than I can put it myself.

Great thoughts cannot have escaped former observation.

Useful truths can be stated in few words.

The origin of all mankind is the same.

Humility is the road that leads us to God.

True humility is but a right estimate of ourselves as God sees us.

Still to the lowly soul God does Himself impart and for His dwelling and His throne chooses the pure in heart.

It is never too late to repent.

The sufficiency of my merit is to know that my merit is not sufficient.

Grace humbles us without degrading and exalts us without inflating us.

Be honest, confess your sins to God and you will not need a psychiatrist.

Look in the mirror to see the person from whom you have most reason to guard yourself.

The most secret thoughts of millions of humans are naked and open before Christ.

If I have not a contrite heart, God's mercy will never be mine.

If God had not manifested mercy in Christ, I could not have a contrite heart.

It takes humility to acknowledge sin and the grace of God to correct it.

The truest conquest is where the soul is bringing every thought into captivity—to the obedience of Christ.

Except you be converted and become as a little child, you cannot enter the kingdom of heaven.

It is easy to deceive oneself without perceiving it.

No man was ever so much deceived by another as by himself.

Self-love is the greatest of flatterers.

> Two went to pray?
> Or rather say
> One went to brag,
> The other to pray;
> Know yourself.

Think often of your own sins and you shall be lenient with the sins of others.

Think of your own faults the first part of the night when you are awake, and of the faults of others the latter part of the night when you are asleep.

A person's holiness can be measured by the degree of his humility.

Deliver me, O Lord, from that evil man, myself.

Every man is his own greatest dupe.

The most humble most easily enter God's kingdom.

Don't be like the man who thought the only time he was wrong was the time he thought he was, and wasn't.

> God of all grace, make us poor in spirit, that ours may be the kingdom of heaven. Give us this Christian grace of humility, the foundation on which all the other graces are laid, the soil in which all the fruit of the Spirit grows.

Strip me of myself, and give me Thyself, O Lord.

He that well and rightly considers his own works will find little cause to judge harshly of another's.

Most of our censure of others is only our desire for self-praise.

True wisdom is to know what is best worth knowing and to do what is best worth doing.

Wisdom is the right use of knowledge.

> . . . get wisdom: and with all thy getting get
> understanding.
> Proverbs 4:7

One pound of learning requires ten pounds of common sense to apply it.

May we learn of life and profit from every experience.

To be wise is to know how little can be known.

It is a point of wisdom to know that we do not know.

One part of knowledge consists in being ignorant of such things as are not worthy to be known.

A knowledge of our own ignorance is the first step toward true knowledge.

If you have knowledge, apply it; if you do not have it, confess your ignorance.

The desire for knowledge increases with the acquisition.

To know the laws of God and to bring our wills into harmony with God's laws is education.

After all, man knows mighty little and may someday learn enough of his own ignorance to fall down and pray.

Better to know only a little and act than to know much and do nothing.

It is easy to learn something about everything but difficult to learn everything about anything.

We can be taught by a child or even an enemy.

Every person you meet knows something worth knowing better than yourself.

He that is taught only by himself has a fool for a teacher.

Dare to be a man of one idea. Have a great one which overshadows all your other aims—an overmastering purpose.

We know accurately only when we know little.

Thoroughly to teach another is the best way for you to learn.

Our chief wisdom is to know our sins and confess them to God and repent.

Life is but one continual course of instruction.

The purest ore is produced from the hottest furnace.

To be proud of learning is a great ignorance.

Truth, like beauty, is never so glorious as when it is plainest.

> Speak your truth quietly and clearly.
> Listen to others—they have a story.
>
> Open my eyes that they may see beauty.
> Open my ears that they may hear truth.

Do not despise nor oppose what you do not understand.

Beware of half-truth, for you may have gotten hold of the wrong half.

The rich depend upon the poor and the poor depend upon the rich.

Prosperity is a great teacher; adversity is greater.

After crosses and losses, people grow humbler and wiser.

Flattery is the food of fools.

The only benefit of flattery is that by hearing what we are not, we may be taught what we ought to be.

Truly, this world can get on without me, if I would but think so.

If I could only see how small a vacancy my death would leave, I would think less of the place I occupy.

> Be not wise in thine own eyes . . . .
> Proverbs 3:7

Guard against that vanity which courts a compliment or is fed by it.

Say little or nothing about yourself.

When you have money in your pocket you are wise and handsome and you sing well, too. Or had you noticed?

Flatterers are the worst kind of enemies.

Abhor the lie that flatters.

> . . . meddle not with him that flattereth with his lips.
> Proverbs 20:19

It's times like these I wish I had more schoolin'—I don't know if you are braggin' on me or makin' fun of me.

Consider your end.

Dust is drawing near to dust.

Seventy is not a sin.

A person would certainly not live to be seventy or eighty years old if this longevity had no meaning for the species to which he belongs.

To grow old is to pass from passion to compassion.

Many a flower blooms unseen and apparently wastes its sweetness on the desert air.

> Thus let me live, unseen, unknown;
> then unlamented let me die;
> steal from the world, and not a stone
> to tell where I lie.

Those of whom we speak least on earth are probably the best known in heaven.

We are but stewards of what we falsely call our own.

Be yourself. Ape no greatness.

Some must follow, and some command, though all are made of clay.

If we fasten our attention on what we have rather than on what we lack, very little wealth is sufficient.

It is fortunate to come of distinguished ancestry.

Better to be nobly remembered than nobly born.

Mere family never made a man great.

Consider not yourself honored because of your father.

A fool may have his coat embroidered with gold, but it is a fool's coat still.

The greatest things are accomplished by individuals.

More heroism has been displayed in the home than on the battlefield.

The owner should be an ornament to the house, and not the house to the owner.

Life is a circle. Hundreds have a share in what I am and do.

A man of stature does not need status.

What one is in little things, he is also in great.

True humility is to attempt great works for God.

> . . . [God] taketh not pleasure in the legs of a man.
> Psalms 147:10

Profit by the mistakes of others. You won't live long enough to make all of the mistakes yourself.

It is easy to find fault with those whose duties you need not face and whose problems you need not solve.

The certain way to be cheated is to fancy oneself more cunning than others.

The empty vessel makes the greatest sound.

Diplomacy is the art of letting someone else have your way.

If life begins at forty, it is because a wise man has lost his conceit by the time he is forty.

Since you are not sure of a minute, throw not away an hour.

This day only is ours.

My memory is the thing I forget with. (A child's definition.)

Quarrels would never last long if the fault were only on one side.

He censures God who quarrels with imperfection.

> What's the use to criticize?
> What's the use to knock?
> What's the use to ridicule?
> Or at some to throw a rock?
> There's none of us that's perfect.
> There's few of us that stay
> And never stray or wander
> From the straight and narrow way.

I'm not perfect—but I'm close.

I wouldn't want to belong to any club that would have me for a member.

There is a noble forgetfulness—that which does not remember injuries.

Our first duty is to forgive.

My decision is maybe—and that's final.

You cannot think my thoughts, speak my words, do my works.

The entire ocean is affected by a pebble.

Nothing so well becomes the true feminine beauty as simplicity.

Women are perfectly well aware that the more they seem to obey the more they rule.

May I use praise as material for humility.

### Where Shall I Work?

Father, where shall I work today?
    And my love flowed warm and free.
Then He pointed me toward a tiny spot
    And said, "Tend that for Me."
I answered quickly, "Oh, no, not that!
    Why, no one would ever see,
No matter how well my work is done;
    Not that little place for me!"
And the word He spoke, it was not stern;
    He answered me tenderly:
"Ah, little one, search that heart of thine.
    Art thou working for them or Me?
Nazareth was a little place,
    And so was Galilee."

*Words of*
**Silver**
*and* **Gold**

# Temperance

*Papa said—*

In Love, Joy, Peace, Long-suffering, Goodness, Gentleness, Meekness, Faith, and Temperance is no excess—neither man nor angel can come into a danger by too much.

Most proverbs are drawn from experence and most are true.

As soon as we learn what to do with thoughts they become our own.

We need not so much to be informed as reminded.

Men of intemperate minds cannot be free—their passions forge their fetters.

If truth be not diffused, error will be.

No violent extremes are lasting—only moderation is secure.

Some of the best principles if pushed to excess can degenerate into fatal vices.

The sternness of justice is but one step removed from the severity of oppression.

Too much generosity leads to extravagance.

The virtue of prosperity is temperance.

Strive to obtain perpetual change and change itself will become monotonous.

If water chokes, what will you drink after it?

All extremes are error.

Extreme heat and extreme cold kill.

You are free if the truth makes you free—otherwise you are a slave.

Excess generally causes reaction and produces a change in the opposite direction.

Nothing too much.

Be an economist in prosperity—you will be one in adversity.

It is mere madness to live like a wretch that you may die rich.

Economy is too late at the bottom of the purse.

The worst place in all the world to live is just beyond your income.

Borrowing is not much better than begging.

He that would have a short Lent, let him borrow money to be repaid at Easter.

What maintains one vice would bring up two children.

A small leak will sink a great ship.

It is not so hard to earn money as to spend it well.

There are two times in a man's life when he should not gamble; when he can't afford it and when he can.

It requires more wit to preserve a fortune than to acquire it.

Poverty is the lack of what is necessary.

No man is poor unless his expenses exceed his resources.

If you would know the value of money, try to borrow some.

The wise use of money is the only advantage there is in having it.

Possess money but be not possessed by it.

You cannot bring about prosperity by discouraging thrift.

If money is not your servant, it will be your master.

What this country needs is a good one-hundred-cents dollar.

Though the people should support the government, the government should not support the people.

He who is master of himself and exists upon his own resources is a noble man.

The rich may have the humility of the poor, and the poor may have the magnanimity of the rich.

We often excuse our own want of philanthropy by giving the name of fanaticism to the more ardent zeal of others.

An executive is a man who goes from his air-conditioned office in an air-conditioned car to his air-conditioned club to take a steam bath.

In law nothing is certain but the expense.

Going to law is losing a cow for the sake of a cat.

> . . . if any man will sue thee at the law, and take away thy coat, let him have thy cloke also.
> Matthew 5:40

The way to have nothing to give is to give nothing.

> A man there was, and they called him mad;
> The more he gave, the more he had.

Pay as you go.

Learn to say "No."

The art of conversation consists as much in listening politely as in talking agreeably.

Recipes for the best speeches should always include shortening.

Brevity is a great charm of eloquence.

The more a person says, the less people remember.

Do not say a little in many words, but a great deal in a few.

Have something to say; say it, and stop when you've said it.

It takes a baby about two years to learn to talk. It takes him fifty or more years to learn to keep his mouth shut.

The secret of being a bore is not to leave anything out.

You can learn more by listening than you can by talking.

> We never know
> To what one little word may grow.

> All gossip has a starting seed,
> And be it large or small
> It may not be the early deed
> That is the worst of all.
> Perhaps the little word *you* said
> Has caused another sorrow
> Or has some other person led
> To add a word tomorrow.

I don't spread gossip—it's the folks I tell who do.

Whenever you are wrong, admit it;
Whenever you are right, shut up.

As we must render an account of every idle word, so we must of our idle silence.

If wisdom's ways you widely seek,
Five things observe with care:
Of whom you speak, to whom you speak,
and how, and when, and where.

. . . If any man offend not in word, the same is a perfect man, and able also to bridle the whole body.

James 3:2

. . . let not the sun go down upon your wrath.

Ephesians 4:26

Chain anger, lest it chain you.

Take not up in anger what you lack in reason.

Anger is like throwing a stone at a wasps' nest.

When you are right, you can afford to keep your temper.
When you are wrong, you can't afford to lose it.

To act while angry is like going to sea in a storm.

A good remedy for anger is delay.

Distance lends enchantment to the view.

It is not what we read but what we remember that educates us.

> When you are the anvil, bear.
> When you are the hammer, strike.

Lose not by overrunning.

Can you kill time without injuring eternity?

He who neglects the present moment throws away all that he has.

Abstain and sustain.

Intemperance is the mother of disease.

Too much food is a vanity. Enough food is a feast.

Reason should direct and appetite obey.

Choose rather to punish your appetites than to be punished by them.

Eat to live, not live to eat.

The stomach begs and clamors and listens to no precepts.

The stomach has a longer memory than the mind.

Give your stomach only what you owe, and not
all you can.

Stick with that diet, and you'll soon win that no-belly
prize.

Continued temperance sustains the body for the longest
period of time.

No man is great that is not master of himself.

Habit is the deepest law of human nature.

Any act oft repeated soon forms a habit.

All of us are more or less slaves to habit.

Bad habits take few holidays.

Wine has drowned more than the sea.

The sight of a drunkard is a better sermon against that
vice than the best that was ever preached on the subject.

No person ever suddenly arrived at the summit of vice.

Teach your children right habits and their future life is safe.

Abstinence is easier for some than temperance.

Be not a slave to yourself.

To will and not to do when there is opportunity is in reality not to will.

The promptings of God are not heard or heeded if life is too busy.

Life is short, but is shorter because of waste of time.

We cry out when we have only a little pain. We smile little for our many blessings.

We cannot bear to be always employed either in duties or meditation without relaxation.

Eve, with all the fruits of Eden blest, except one, rather than leave that one unknown, lost all the rest.

Many are striking at the branches of evil, few at the root.

No man can be temperate who regards pleasure as the highest good.

The habit of saving is itself an education; it fosters every virtue, teaches self-denial, and cultivates the sense of order.

Few persons have sufficient wisdom to prefer censure, which is useful, to praise, which deceives us.

In the world a man lives in his own age; in solitude in all ages.

An optimist is one who can always see the bright side of the other fellow's problems.

Use pleasures as material for temperance.

Nations have boundary lines and farms have fences.

Know where your freedom ends and the freedom of your neighbor begins.

Your rights end at the end of my nose.

Give not thought to what is good for one group without thinking what is good for all.

Freedom without the wise discharge of its coexisting responsibilities imperils not only the individual, but weakens the entire society.

Put all good eggs in one basket and then watch that basket.

Haste is not always speed.

God gives us flowers and showers.

Nor is a day lived if the dawn be left out of it.

# Faith

*Papa said—*

To have known one good old man helps our faith in God, in ourselves and in each other immeasurably.

The discoveries of ages past belong less to their authors than to those who make them practically useful to the world.

The wisdom of the wise and the experience of ages may be preserved by quotation.

The writings of the wise are the only riches our posterity cannot squander.

By faith we understand—by faith we know.

Understand not that you may believe, but believe that you may understand.

"Impossible"—that's not good English.

Nothing is impossible.

> . . . all things work together for good to them that love God . . . .
>
> Romans 8:28

God overrules all accidents. He brings them and His laws together, and makes them of service to His purpose.

Act upon your impulses, but pray that they may be directed by God.

Men do not avail themselves of the riches of God's grace.

Faith visits us in defeat and disappointment.

God may be had for the asking.

Begin and end your day with God.

A prayer is a wish toward God.

Prayer is not eloquence but earnestness.

I trust God for what I ask.

I believe I shall receive either what I ask, or what I should ask.

I thank God that all my prayers have not been answered.

Never wish your ignorance to overrule God's wisdom.

We do not pray in faith if we think we know better than God.

God gives the very best to those who leave the choice with Him.

Prayer is offering up our desires unto God for things agreeable to His will, in the Name of Christ, with confession of our sins and thankful acknowledgment of His mercies.

God denies a Christian nothing but with a design to grant him something better.

> He that turneth away his ear from hearing the law, even his prayer shall be abomination.
> Proverbs 28:9

God hears only what the heart speaks.

Prayer without watching is hypocrisy.

You never seek in vain.

Every act of duty is an act of faith.

I should trust in God as if God did all, and yet labor as earnestly as if I myself did all.

Learn to work and wait.

There are times when our strength is to wait.

There is not a moment without some duty.

Do the duty nearest you first and the second will seem clearer.

Do today's duty.

Perish discretion when it interferes with duty.

Fulfill the claims of today.

Duty and today are ours.

Results and the future belong to God.

Be faithful to the duties of the present and God will provide for the future.

Faith rests on the promises of God.

In the greatest danger, faith says, "I have a great God."

What we desire may not be good for us.

What we would avoid may be essential to our well-being.

As God wills; what God wills; when God wills.

This is best which God sends; it is His will; it is mine.

> To do or not to do;
> To have or not to have,
> I leave to Thee.
> Thy will be done in me.

Faith does not come from feeling, but feeling from faith—the less we feel, the more we should trust.

> Trust in the Lord with all thine heart; and lean not unto thine own understanding. In all thy ways acknowledge him, and he shall direct thy paths.
>
> Proverbs 3:5, 6

Do we deny God in our deed?

Faith, if not transformed into character, has lost its power.

Make your decision as wisely as possible after praying for wisdom, and then forget it.

Breathe deeply in faith.

Bind together all the affairs of life, great and small, and turn them over to God.

Life is a constant want and should be a constant prayer.

> Who trusts in God's unchanging love
> Builds on the rock that naught can move.

There is nothing too great for God to accomplish.

There is nothing too small for Him to attend to.

To Him who sits supreme, let us commit the hour, the day, the year, and fearless view the whole.

Hope waits.

Faith dares.

Outside the will of God there can be no true success; in the will of God there can be no real failure.

Play fast and loose with faith.

There is no substitute for prayer.

Faith is vital.

I cannot have a need my God cannot supply.

Feed your faith. Starve your doubts.

To be an atheist requires an infinitely greater measure of faith than to receive all the great truths which atheists would deny.

God never wrought miracles to convince atheism because His ordinary works convince.

To deny God is for the thing formed to say that nothing formed it; and that which made it is not.

The fool hath said in his heart, There is no God . . . .
Psalms 14:1

The Gospel was first seen and known in Jesus before we were able to read it in The Book.

The Gospel is good news—the only hope for a world seemingly bent on self-destruction.

Some people believe chance could have made the world, when they know it cannot build a house.

Belief in the Bible influences the actions of my life.

Believe what the Bible tells you, and do what the Bible bids you.

I believe the Gospel is the only remedy for our nation's troubles as well as my own.

Ask not where God is—but where He is not.

While reason is puzzling itself about mystery, faith is turning it to daily bread, feeding on it in her heart.

God governs in the affairs of men.

Duties are ours—events are God's.

In the glass of things temporal see the image of things spiritual.

For the need of today we have corresponding strength given.

Don't knock it until you've tried it.

Our only hope is in the mercy of God through Jesus Christ.

Faith experiences things which we cannot see, hear, touch, taste or smell.

Find the first right thread to pull and the whole of our tangled problem begins to unravel.

Do I believe all that God teaches?

Do I endeavor to do all He commands?

God still speaks to those who take time to listen.

The holiest sanctuary is home.

There is only one time that is important, and that is now.

The time for seeking God is always now.

King of Kings, yet born of Mary!

There is hope for the most careless of prodigals and the most abandoned of sinners.

Unto Whom all hearts are open, all desires known and from Whom no secrets are hid.

'Twas a sheep, not a lamb, that wandered away
In the parable Jesus told.
If the sheep go wrong, it will not be long
Till the lambs are as wrong as they.

The faith that comes from conflict may become the strongest.

Examine the evidences of Christianity and dwell not on the vices and imperfections of professing Christians.

No man ever repented of being a Christian on his deathbed.

Place not your trust in this present world.

The amplest knowledge has the largest faith.

I sought God at a distance, not knowing He is near.

I sought Him abroad in His world and behold, He was in me.

Jesus became as we are that we may become as He is.

What is true is not new.

A changeless Christ for a changing world!

He who has God lacks nothing.

Man knows mighty little. May we someday learn enough of our own ignorance to fall down and pray.

There are many deceitful bypaths, most of which lead to precipices and pits.

Keep your doubts to yourself—I have enough of my own.

Reading The Old Book over, there we find the light to which we long have been so blind.

The Bible will stand a thousand readings; and he who has gone over it most frequently is the surest of finding new wonders there.

A stitch in time saves nothing unless your needle is threaded.

Gladly committing ourselves, body and soul, utterly and completely to God is the beginning of really living the abundant life.

Are you the foolish person who thinks it is in your power to commit more sin than God can forgive?

> I, even I, am he that blotteth out thy transgressions for mine own sake, and will not remember thy sins.
> Isaiah 43:25

Why keep rehearsing something that even God has refused to remember? At times it is much harder to forgive ourselves than it is for the Lord to forgive us. We need only to simply acknowledge that we are sinners and accept Jesus as our Saviour. Do not complicate what the Lord has made clear enough for a child to comprehend.

Let God have your life. He can do more with it than you can.

Cast all your care on God. That anchor holds.

> I come to Thee with empty hands—
> The surer to be filled from Thine.
>
> Divine Instructor, gracious Lord,
> Be forever near;
> Teach me to love Your sacred Word
> And view my Saviour there.

The Bible is the Word of God, containing all things necessary to salvation.

Thy Word is truth.

Every truth in the universe agrees with all others.

Truth crushed to earth will rise again.

Science is seeking after God through the study of His ways.

Time is powerless against truth.

God's Word needs none of man's explanation. The Holy Spirit can explain to each heart.

Those who listen for the voice of truth will hear.

> God is so high you can't get above Him.
> God is so low you can't get beneath Him.
> God is so wide you can't get around Him.
> You'd better come in by the Door.

A practicing Christian who asks whether he has time for prayer is like a carpenter asking whether he has time to sharpen his tools.

When we pray we link ourselves with the inexhaustible Motive Power that spins the universe.

Prayer is practicing the presence of God.

We can pray everywhere.

True prayer is a way of life.

Prayer is first and foremost a practice in honesty.

What God has promised, He is able and willing to perform.

But my God shall supply all your need according to his riches in glory by Christ Jesus.

Philippians 4:19

To every honest question Jesus has the answer.

No creaturely need is outside the scope of prayer.

We cannot fall below the arm of God, howsoever low it be we fall.

Understanding is the wages of a lively faith, and faith is the reward of a humble ignorance.

Faith makes the discords of the present the harmonies of the future.

Faith makes all evil good to us, and all good better.

Faith draws the sting out of every trouble.

Faith takes the bitterness out of every affliction.

Jesus is the foundation of our hope, the object of our faith, the subject of our love, and the model of our conduct.

God writes the Gospel not in the Bible alone, but on trees, flowers, clouds and stars.

Hear the Word reverently and regularly. Obey it fervently without reservation, hesitation or qualification.

Live a life totally committed in thought, word and deed to the precepts and principles of the Bible.

But be ye doers of the word, and not hearers only . . . .
                                                    James 1:22

>     Words without the heart
>     Our God will never hear;
>     Nor will He to those lips attend
>     Where prayers are not sincere.

I do not fear to tread the path I do not see,
Because the hand of One who loves is leading me.

>     Father, in Thy hands and keeping,
>     Now I place all my affairs,
>     Every little situation,
>     All my little tasks and cares,
>     All my loved ones, fully knowing
>     They can neither fail nor fall.
>     They are in Thy sure protection
>     While Thy love encircles all.

In this joyous reassurance,
I relinquish worry thought.
From my shoulders loads are lifted.
I accept Thy Truth as taught;
Just to cast on Thee the burden
And no longer be afraid,
To behold Thy prompt salvation,
To depend upon Thine aid.

Prayer is as essential as eating and sleeping.

God controls every atom of the universe.

God is the power that creates the rose, a human cell, a continent, an ocean and all the natural laws which regulate everything from the blood stream to the heavenly bodies.

God knows our thoughts, faults, desires and needs no matter what we say or how we say it.

God is nearer to me than I am myself.

When God closes a door, look for another He has opened.

"No gain!" I said, but I forgot
My Father's faithful Word,
That all things work for blessing here
To them that love the Lord.

Many lives that seem marred by accident are in the process of being made by Providence.

You are not required to complete the task. You are not permitted to lay it down.

The will of God will never lead you where the grace of God cannot keep you.

The rains will fall—the winds will blow—we are not building on the shifting sands, but on a rock—THE ROCK, CHRIST.

> O Thou Whose bounty fills my cup,
> With every blessing meet;
> We give Thee thanks for every drop,
> The bitter and the sweet.
> We thank Thee for the desert road,
> And for the riverside;
> For all the goodness Thou hast bestowed,
> For all we've been denied.
>
> His eye forsees our greatest good,
> While we at best are weak;
> And thus in wisdom He withholds
> The boon that oft we seek.
> And yet His all-sufficient grace
> He bids us freely share;
> And in a way we little know,
> The Lord will answer prayer.

I prayed: the answer, though deferred,
Brought not the thing I sought.
He answered better than my plea—
Aye, better than my thought.

A Christian is pleased with everything that happens, because he knows it could not happen unless it had first pleased God, and that which pleases Him must be the best.

If we trust God as we should, we can live above anxiety for earthly needs.

Submission to God is the only balm that can heal the wound He gives us.

The Lord's Prayer teaches us what to ask of God—how to pray.

Once I sought a time and place for solitude and prayer; but now where'er I find Thy face, I find a closet there.

. . . when thou prayest, enter into thy closet, and when thou hast shut thy door, pray to thy Father which is in secret . . . .

Matthew 6:6

God's word is the greatest of all books, and its Author is the greatest of all teachers.

The Author of the Bible is the Holy Spirit. When you study the Bible, you are being instructed by a divine teacher.

The elect are whosoever will.

The non-elect are whosoever won't.

There are no hopeless situations. There are only people who have grown hopeless about them.

> . . . let God be true, but every man a liar . . . .
> Romans 3:4

Bless God for what you have and trust Him for what you need.

Think of death not as ending, but as life beginning.

When Death whispers, "You must go from earth," hear Christ saying, "You are coming to Me."

We do not believe in immortality because we have proved it, but we forever try to prove it because we believe it.

In the desire for immortality we feel we have sure proof of our capacity for it.

> Since God has made this world so fair,
> Where sin and death abound,
> How beautiful beyond compare
> Will paradise be found.

I am conscious of eternal life.

Our yearnings are homesickness for heaven.

If there were no future life, our souls would not thirst for it.

If I die, I shall be with God; if I live, He will be with me.

As long as we live, God will give us living grace, and He will give us dying grace when it is time to die.

Thy Word, O God, is the fountain of life eternal and passes not away.

There is no death. Did Jesus not say, "I die that you may live always"?

Thanks to that Gospel which opens the vision of an endless life.

Our dying is as wonderful as our living, for both have become in Christ the entrance to a larger life.

Living is death; dying is life.

When, with bowed head,
And silent, streaming tears,
With mingled hopes and fears,
To earth we yield our dead;
The saints, with clearer sight,
Do cry in glad accord—
"A soul released from prison
Is risen, is risen—
Is risen to the glory of the Lord."

The leaves in autumn fall when the fruit is ripened and their work is done. Falling is their graceful and beautiful surrender of life when they have finished their summer of offering service to God and man. The great lesson the fall of the leaf teaches is do your work well, and then be ready to depart when God calls.

Our birth is our death begun.

A little work, a little sleep, a little love and it's all over.

Life is a journey, not a home.

The truest end of life is to know that it never ends.

The end of life is to be like God.

. . . we shall be like him; for we shall see him as he is.
1 John 3:2

He that lives to live forever never fears dying.

> O death, where is thy sting? O grave, where is thy victory?
>
> 1 Corinthians 15:55

> Yea, though I walk through the valley of the shadow of death, I will fear no evil: for thou art with me . . . .
>
> Psalms 23:4

Dying to the Christian is the way of life eternal.

> Is your place a small place?
> Tend it with care;
> God set you there.
> Is your place a large place?
> Guard it with care;
> God set you there.
> Whatever your place, it is not yours alone,
> But God's who set you there.

The faith that saves issues is good works.

The faith which does not manifest itself in works is no true faith in Christ.

Give and to you shall be given—not receive and then give.

There is nothing insignificant—nothing.

A hair can live for centuries.

A brick can last three thousand years.

A change of jobs is not necessary. Stay where you are and do a better job, be a better citizen, live a better life.

God does nothing or permits nothing to be done but what you would do yourself, if you could see through all events or things as well as He.

Every asker receives, every seeker finds—not necessarily what he asks or seeks.

If we would obtain exactly what we ask, we must make our wills God's will and ask only for things we know God is willing to give. He knows better than we what is best for us.

> I dare not pray
> For winds to waft me on my way,
> But leave it to a higher will
> To stay, or speed me, trusting still
> That all is well and sure that He
> Who launched my boat will sail with me,
> Through storm and calm, and will not fail
> Whatever breezes may prevail,
> To land me, every peril past,
> Within His sheltering haven at last.

### The Evolutionist's Answer

As the evolutionist sat with his son upon his knee,
  "Tell of the beginning," was the fellow's plea.

So the scholar with his learning and diploma on the wall,
  quoted from his textbooks all he could recall.

"In the beginning there was nothing but a little bit of gas,
  but it finally got together and made a lot of mass.

"Now where the gas had come from and how it came about,
is not discussed by scholars, it's taken without doubt.

"When the elements cooled off and the gasses caused their strife,
all of a sudden life sprung up, from where there was no life.

"At first of course there was but fish by ocean tossed and thrown,
then some decided they would walk, so legs and feet were grown.

"Others decided they'd like to fly up in the heaven blue,
  they wished so hard that soon it seems, wings had sprouted thru.

"Finally apes began to think, with brains they decided to grow.
The smartest one became a man—natural selection, you know."

As he ended his wise discourse and glanced at the lad
    upon his knee,
'twas hard for the simple minded lad to understand, he
    could see.

Then as if in defense of his cause, the scholar said with a
    nod,
"If you don't believe this just happened by chance, then
    you have to believe there's a God."

BILL E. SMITH

**Words of**
**Silver**
*(and)* **Gold**

*Papa said—*

> Good words
> Right words
> Sound words

Easily remembered and always ready for use

> I repeat what is old—
> mine by conquest—and they
> can be yours also.

**DATE DUE**

| | | |
|---|---|---|
| | | |
| | | |
| | | |
| | | |
| | | |
| | | |
| | | |

Petty, Jo                                          242.
AUTHOR                                             4
Words of Silver and Gold                           PET
TITLE

| DATE DUE | BORROWER'S NAME |
|---|---|
| | |
| | |
| | |
| | |

Petty, Jo                                          242.
Words of Silver and Gold                           4
                                                   PET

*Words of*
**Silver**
*(and* **Gold**

*Papa said—*

> Good words
> Right words
> Sound words

Easily remembered and always ready for use

> I repeat what is old—
> mine by conquest—and they
> can be yours also.